Tranquility in a ___

place.

Life in the system.

BY Zane Hunt.

Contents page

Chapter 13, institutionalization.

Introduction.

In this book I will talk to the reader as a survivor of both mental health and addiction, hopefully giving the reader a lived insight to what it's like to be in a continuous battle with yourself and the impact this thus has on our loved ones and our quality of life.

Having spent 20 years in prison, and mental health hospital's up and down the country without a choice and a unheard voice hopefully this book will both inspire, and help readers from all walks of life, and give them ways of coping with difficulties that life throws at them, from what seems every angle, and also professionals a brief look at what it's like to be on the receiving hand of some at times outdated treatment methods and beneficial ways in which I found particularly helpful and were effective on myself.

Finally, I would like to take this opportunity to thank some very important people that helped myself along my journey.

My mother Amanda has always been a very supportive person in my life who at times would of been easier for her to walk away, and give up on me, but she never has she has visited me in all areas of the country in prisons and hospitals always with a smile on her face when to be honest this must of been very difficult to see her eldest son throwing his life away as I did. Life has

always been tough for my mum, often going without herself to make sure we had food on the table, clothes trainers and giving us the best life, she could when it must have seemed at times like I had put myself on a vicious, downward and destructive path.

To my stepdad Robert Jones, thank you for all the support, mates.

My little brothers Scott and Luke I'm proud to have you as my brothers, and I'm sorry for not always showing it especially Scott you saved my life and I know the final decision you had to make wouldn't have been easy for you, but I literally would not be here if you didn't make that decision thank you, you little shit I do love you and there aren't words powerful enough to express how sorry I am for putting you through what I did when I was on that satanic drug, monkey dust. Love you bro.

My psychologist in Ashworth high secure, thank you for building up my confidence and allowing myself to be.

more open and not giving up on me when others around me were. (Thank you Louise)

Ashleigh Fallon for taking me through my trauma word EMDR and sitting with myself in police interviews fighting my corner.

While at the final stage of my journey Ray, Vick, Matt, Nicki, Sam and Chloe, Lisa, and Tony for not giving up on me while at the Hatherton Centre and trying your hardest to get me back on track and live my life.

My gym instructor marc for never giving up on me getting me into the gym when some days I'd rather have stayed in bed, getting me in shape again, (not forgetting what you did for your crown and its people serving this country you're a true hero).

Kelsey, Brandon, and Bella for all the support over the years and still to this day I love you all very dearly. You've all been a blessing.

My Auntie Geraldine, and cousins Wayne and Paula.

Mujahid and Marcus for always being there

whenever I need to chat or for advice Insha'Allah, I can repay the

favor to you both, we've been in some bad situations, and in some bad institutions together but we've always kept it together, no matter how much the system has tried to beat us.

My solicitor Tom, no doubt got me out of a

system I was trapped in.
Thanks Tom you're a
legend.

To my grandad Gerald
and my grandmother
Rita although we don't
see each other any
longer and our spirits are
worlds apart our bonds
are eternal. I love and
miss you both dearly
(gone but never
forgotten).

Finally, I would like to
thank ALLAH,
Alhamdulillah for making
me a better person

spiritually, mentally, and physically Masha 'ALLAH I give thanks.

ZANE HUNT.

<u>Chapter 1.</u>

Battling demons head on.

Try to imagine that one day you awoke from a nightmare sweating, shaking and terrified. Now imagine that you haven't actually woke from this nightmare and you are trapped in a pitch black cave scrambling desperately trying to free yourself, in the far distance you can see a peak of light, but the closer you get the further away it seems, then just as you begin to reach the light you come across a demon terrifying in appearance. First you try fighting but it's too strong, then you try running but it's too fast, then you allow yourself to take a step back, breath, regain focus and some mental resilience and

the demon see's this
and realizes even for a
demon of its size you
are in fact too strong,
then it bows down and
allows you to walk into
the light, this may.

only for a short time
and you may find
yourself battling that
demon again but
remember the mental
strength that beat it the
first time can and will
help you again.

The story I have just
told would seem a
nightmare for some, but
for some people it is
often a reality who are
on a daily basis battling
demons, and often feel
as though the
nightmare will never
end, but it's important
to remember the mental
strength that got you
out of that nightmare
the first time can and
will help you again, and
each time you will
become stronger and
more able to deal with

whatever demon life throws at you.

When you feel as though you are in a place where you feel like quitting, push through where most.

people quit, adapt you way of approaching difficult situations and strategize your ways in which you think and deal with life trial, and tribulations "you re the master of your own happiness."

Don't lose, win or learn!!!!!!!!!!!!!

Chapter "2. A traumatic day.

I remember going to the beach whilst on holiday with family, friends and loved ones. Whilst at the beach there was a high tide and the water unexpectedly burst its banks and started to engulf the nearby town. My loved ones and I began to run to high ground but as I was running away, I got my foot stuck in a manhole, I was terrified and was trying to set myself free, but I was unable to do so, my family friends the people I cared for the most were.

witnessing myself battle
this terrifying ordeal
and living every second
of it with me.

After a short while the
emergency services
attended to try and set
me free.my loved ones
could see the
predicament I was in,
and they could see how
scared I was and they
along with the
emergency services.

we're screaming at me
trying to tell me what to
do in order to set
myself free, but I
couldn't focus and
Before long I couldn't
hold on any longer and
the water drowned me,
whilst everyone who
cared for me the most
witnessed the whole
thing before their eyes.

On reflection I should
have just cut the leg off.
This may sound
extreme but if I did, I
would have been set

free and not putting myself or my loved ones through what I did.

The story I have told is that of a metaphorical one and my foot getting stuck in a manhole is symbolic of things that hold us back in life, that could be a relationship, trauma , addiction a feeling whatever it is that may be holding us back the best thing no matter how hard it is to cut it off and move on.

If like in the story you find something holding you back in life from being happy cut it off throw it away,

Move on and be happy, everyone deserves to be happy even YOU so don't allow past traumas or addictions, or negative thoughts hold you back from being happy, cut it off, and try to rebuild

yourselves into the people we all want to be.
BELIEVE AND YOU CAN ACHIEVE, BELIEVE IN YOURSELF AND YOU'LL BE UNSTOPPABLE!!!!!

Chapter 3.

Be mindful not to allow your mind to wander.

Try to imagine to yourself, that you are standing on a busy platform at a busy Train station. Now try to imagine that the trains are going past at a Thousand miles an hour, only in view for a split second before passing by. You could either jump on the train or go.

on a journey without quite knowing where the journey ends, or you can just let the Train pass.

The Trains at the station resemble your thoughts, and you can get on the Train and ride the thought or you can just let it pass, and bring yourself back to the present, and not ruminate on the thought and take yourself into places that are scary and uncomfortable, often leading us to feel out of control, emotionally, physically and mentally, feeling anxious and afraid of what's to come.

As humans we fear the unknown, and when we fear the unknown, and allow our thoughts and minds to wander we begin to catastrophize. By allowing yourself to catastrophize you begin to think irrationally, often leading to us to act out of the ordinary and to lose control of yourself and the situation you are in.

There is no need to fear the unknown; it hasn't happened yet and probably never will, just as you allow the trains on the platform at the station to pass by and allow your thoughts to do the same. Try to focus on your breath or something you can see, and every time your mind begins to wander and ruminate, bring yourself back your breath or whatever it is you are focusing on, allow the thought to pass, and as the train's do on the platform they will pass. Be mindful of yourself and your surroundings.

Mindfulness is a Buddhist philosophy that allows the mind and the body to be (one), connecting its bodily experiences with reality. If the body mediates between both mind and reality then it shows in the above, then it's through the experience of the body that we can ease anxieties and find clarity in Yourself.

 Mindfulness was first developed 2500 years ago by Buddhist monks, and was introduced into the western world in 1979 as a holistic way of treating people with both physical and psychological traumas and pain.

Today mindfulness is used by people all over the world known as the mindfulness movement.

Chapter 4.

Dear depression.

Dear depression, all those nights you would keep me awake scared of what's to come, all the day's week's, and years you took from me my childhood, my happiness, all the times you told me to kill myself I nearly got killed for that, all of the lie's that you told me that I wasn't good enough, somebody told me I was, all the times you told me nobody cared somebody told me they did. I demand a refund on every lie that you sold me.

and I'm announcing now that the devil can't control me. You are a fake coward who hides in the shadows preying on your victims' vulnerabilities. It just took me a while to realize you weren't my friend. Now I want you to look in the mirror and see what I used to see as a scared boy, and cry at the shame that it brings you, and be too afraid to open.

Finally, I want to tell you I forgive you; you made me stronger and more willed to strive for a better life!!!

Yours sincerely Zane.

The letter I have just written is to a fake friend I have lived with through my whole life. He took me to some dark places; I remember being in long term.

segregation in a maximum-security facility Ashworth in Liverpool, and there was a psychologist called Louise who would always visit me in my cell instilling hope within me, helping me through a dark period in my life. Every week she would come and see me and I would dismiss everything she tried to tell for nearly a year, until one day I opened up, and when I did this a small smile came to her face, a smile of joy knowing that finally she had got through to me where everyone else had given up.

After that session she left, I went back to my bed on the floor in my tiny cell and had feelings that were alien to me; they were feelings of happiness and excitement of what was to come. I was on the road to recovery.

No matter how much of a dark place you find yourself in be true to yourself don't be afraid to open up, I was in the highest secure unit in the country, segregated

from others due my
violent behavior but I

found hope in that dark
place, and turned what
some might see as the
end of the road into a
feeling of hope.

Never let thoughts and
feelings control who
you are, it's ok to be
sad in fact it's normal,
it's how we deal with
that emotion that will
determine how it ends.

We all have five core emotion's happiness, sadness, fear, anger, and jealousy. From these five primary emotions we will have a secondary feeling leading us to experience physical sensation's resulting in an action.

The trigger to these emotions is subconscious along with the emotion being subconscious also, but the way in which we respond to the initial thought surrounding the trigger will enable us to illicit a more positive experience of the emotion, leading us to a more positive feeling thus experiencing a less intense physical sensation makes us feel more in

control, and allows us to make better decisions, resulting in a more positive, prosocial response.

Don't be afraid to name and feel the emotion you are experiencing. It's perfectly normal to feel it, as said earlier we all experience these emotions we are biologically pre-dispositioned to do this. Over time nurture yourself into allowing yourself to be less judgmental on how you feel and recognize that it's perfectly normal to feel this way.

Don't be afraid to open
up a problem halved.

Chapter 5.

Addiction.

After going to Prison at 19 and coming out at 35 I was blind to these new synthetic manufactured drugs that were now on the streets.

A new powerful drug called Monkey Dust was now the streets tearing through communities like a cancer,

Monkey dust or "Methylenedioxyphenol pyrrolidinobutiophenone" is a synthetic chemical that increase brain and central nervous system activity in much the same way as amphetamines or MDMA "ecstasy" monkey dust causes the user to have an outer body experience causing the user to feel elated, and delirious.

Monkey dust or any addiction is defined as a chronic, relapsing disorder characterized by drug seeking and use despite adverse consequence, it is a brain disorder, because it involves functional changes to the brain circuit, involved in reward, stress and control.

I was taking bath salts or "monkey dust "for only a short while but the effects were devastating not only for myself but also my loved ones who had to live.

and bear witness to what this drug not only did to me but also to us as a family.

In just a little over a month my mental health had deteriorated drastically along with my physical health and appearance.

The drug over me, my whole life revolved around taking the drug, at times I would not sleep for a week at a time causing severe paranoid thoughts hallucinations and delusions.

It was Christmas 2022, and I was so far gone under the influence of the drug I didn't even realize it was Christmas. I remember my friend Marc picking me.

up in his car, phoning my fiancée and telling her I was in a bad way and that I had been taking the drug. I was too ashamed to face my fiancé and son, so I went into my flat and took an overdose of codeine, before waking up and putting my shame to

one side and going to my family home, I remember the horror on my fiancé's and sons face at what they saw when I walked through the door, to make things worse I honestly thought it was

Christmas eve the gifts were under the tree the table was set only for my family to tell me that it was now 2023 and I had missed Christmas and new year altogether.

A short time after this it got so out of control my mother and stepdad drove 4 hours from Wales to pick me up and take me to their home. Once there I lay on the sofa, my mum's dogs comforting me. I was like a corpse; my

mum ran me a bath my skin was rotting away so bad that it was all left in the bath. I can't remember the journey to my mums, but my little brother Scott sat up all night with me thinking.
I was going to die; he had traveled to Telford to get me safe and back to my mum.

I made videos to all my loved one's not thinking I was going to get through the night. Before this I had passed out in my shed and my little dog Bella had found me and alerted my family, she was amazing as the shed door was closed and she had got through a tiny gap in the side. It's sad some might just think she's just a dog but she is so emotional sometimes she would cry when she saw me the way I was and wouldn't leave my side she is my little sidekick, I have a step son but no biological children of my own and

she really is like my
little daughter.

Eventually I got recalled
to Hospital, my liver
and kidneys were
damaged along with my
brain my skin was
rotten and I smelt of
rotten flesh, I was
coughing up blood, the
detox was hard but not
as hard as what I had
put Kelsey, Brandon,
Scott my Mum and Rob
through and there are

not words powerful to describe how ashamed and sorry I am.

Don't allow people we often see as friends to see as a vulnerability in our personalities, and to use this to their advantage, they are not friends instead fake cowards who disguise themselves as friends. Keep your circle small quality over quantity ".

For Addiction you give up EVERYTHING for ONE thing, in recovery you give up ONE thing for EVERYTHING"!!!!!!!!!

Chapter 6.

A day in the life of an Addict.

A day in my life as a monkey dust addict. As said in the previous chapter this drug took over my whole life, everything evolved around taking it.

Each morning I would wake up in chronic pain not only physically, but emotionally also, I would be sweating, shaking my bones felt as though they were weak and crumbling, but all that was on my mind was having a fix.

Some mornings I
wouldn't

have any dust to hand
so I would be trying to
scrape my pipe just to
at least get something
to ease the pain I was
feeling, I would feel as
though I couldn't
concentrate or function
without a pipe.

Once I had my first pipe of the day I would walk to my dealers " fake friend" and pick up some more dust and the day started all over again, I hated every minute of it I had turned into a junky and unless, and you've been an addict you really can't appreciate how hard it is for both the user, and the family witnessing the demise of their loved one.

I would get my pipe
ready and a spare one,
then fold foil to use on
my pipe, and stash
extra foil in the sole of
my shoe, and a drawing
pin, light ten cigarettes
and burn them not to
smoke but for the ash,
and put this into a little
tub so I had it to hand
to put on my pipe so I
could smoke my dust,
then I would always

have lots of lighters, flints, and a can of gas in case any of them ran out.

My life was out of control. I had lost myself to this drug both physically and mentally. There was a smell of rotten fish coming from my body along with cramps all over my body. Sometimes I would sit in a house smoking for days on end, and not even realize it, it would feel like a few hours, I

would not eat or drink,
just smoking pipe after
pipe.

Sometime before I got
on the dust whilst I was
in prison I developed a
degenerative eye
condition (keratoconus)
affecting my corneas,
and had to have two
corneal transplants, ,my
eyes were still healing
from surgery and when
I got recalled into a
mental health hospital, I
taken to Birmingham
eye hospital because I
had lost majority of the

site in my right eye,
once I had been seen
by an ophthalmic DR
they thought they were
going to have to
remove my right eye as
the cornea was
rejecting and the blood

vessels at the back of
the eye were dying.
This was scary as the
DR told myself if I had
come to the hospital 12
hours later they would
of had no choice but to
remove the eye

altogether, the DR informed me that the monkey dust had caused an infection and I was very lucky I haven't lost my eye, also when I arrived at the mental health hospital my weight had dropped from 85kg to just 65kg, I was coughing up blood, I was passing blood in my urine my feet and legs were flaky and rotting away, once my blood results were back they found my liver and kidneys to be damaged, along with my brain and now suffer with rapid speech, ticks and my pituitary gland is producing too much testosterone. Whilst going through my detox my blood pressure dropped very low when it was taken, it was 60 over 10, just after I collapsed in the corridor the DOCTORS and nurses happened to be having a meeting on the ward at the time and rushed to help, I don't know what would have happened if I had

gone back to prison
rather than hospital and
I was alone in my cell.

There are things I can't
change, and save like
my eye, and my
damaged brain and
also the shame and
guilt I have from being
on this drug and what it
had done to my family
and friends to see me
go from someone who
was in very good shape
physically and mentally
to turning into a drug

addict who people would talk down to but I had to let it go as I relied on these people to get my drugs from, so I went from being respected to being talked to and treated like a piece of shit.

Chapter 7.

The monkey dust community.

There are drug users in every society who take all drugs, but people who take monkey dust have their own community outcast by users of other drugs. People who use monkey dust all seem to be scheming against each other, often coming up with conspiracies about other users, often leading to severe paranoia making the user do things he/she wouldn't usually do, often becoming violent to themselves or other users from the fear

that had manifested
in their minds,
elicited from how this
powerful drug had
effected there
mind's. People
would do anything
for a pipe leading
them to rob each
other, the public, and
from shops to feed
their habit this really
is crushing
communities up and
down the country.
Unfortunately, there

isn't a replacement/treatment for monkey dust as there is for other drugs such as heroin were.

a doctor would prescribe "methadone" there is no chemical compound for monkey dust as is for heroin for instance, so the

users are stuck in a
catch 22 and once
taking the drug it is
almost impossible
for the user to stop,
and users are left in
the dilemma of not
knowing what to do,
often leading them to
sadly take their own
lives as a way out.
Nobody wants to live
the life of an addict
and it's sad that the
government is not
driven enough to do

something about this drug problem; it's not only on the user's their families but also the communities that are also directly affected by this satanic drug.

Chapter 8.

Not everyone you fight is your enemy, & not everyone you think helps you is your friend.

People we often view as friends, often have ulterior motives, and winning our trust

over time will
bring out chinks in
our personalities,
and because of
their callous ways
they will use this
to their gain, often
with a financial
reward for
themselves not
really caring for
the person of
whom they were
taking advantage

of. A person's
greed

overcomes some
who have
achieved so very
little and who
consciously feel
so de-valued in
themselves that
they will both
mirror and project
how shitty they

feel about
themselves onto
someone who
deep down they
wish to be like,
this jealousy
could be of a
desire to have a
relationship they
he/she has or
employment,
friendships etc.,
whatever it is they
know they can't

have it, so they wish to destroy the person's life and bring them down to their biodegradable level, thus giving them a sense of control over their own lives that they have little to none over their own.

Don't allow
others'
insecurities
become yours, let
them live in their
own ruin and by
offering a friend
drugs or anything
harmful this is
only a reflection
of both them and

their pathetic
lives, this does
not reflect you
only them who
subvert pretend to
be our friend
when really they
are far from that,
in fact they are
fake cowards who
hide in the
shadows praying
on vulnerabilities

they see in an individual.

Keep your circle close, and small quality over quantity, stay you, stay true.

Don't pray for an easy life, but instead pray for the strength to endure a difficult one, because life is an uphill battle and shit rolls down hill, we just have to dodge it where we can and avoid getting hit, but if and when we are hit

by shit in life be
resilient, and let it
be our own shit
life throws at us
not someone else
who like I said
drag us down to
their own
insecure level.

When fishermen go crabbing and they put their catch in a bucket, and one crab will try escape but the others drag it back down as so not to allow it to escape, well that's exactly what these low life Monkey dust drug dealers do,

they drag us back
down to their level
because in reality
they see hope in
you, but not in
themselves.

Chapter 9.

Link between
monkey dust
and psychosis.

Monkey dust or "Methylenedioxypheno l pyrrolidinopentiopheno ne" is an ever-growing popular drug that selectively damages brain serotonin. It is most commonly inhaled by smoking the substance. The drug affects three neurotransmitters: in much the same way as "cocaine and MDMA." The three neurotransmitters it affects are, serotonin, dopamine and norepinephrine being released by synaptic vesicles in neurons. This results in increased neurotransmitter activity. Monkey dust use causes mood elevating effects. However, by releasing large amounts of serotonin M.D causes the brain to become significantly depleted, contributing to negative behavioral aftereffects and the user experiences this several days after use. The drug boosts energy levels and produces an intense high like MDMA and COCAINE. Withdrawal from the drug include involuntary body movements, depression, and suicidal thoughts. Long term use causes reduced cortical gray matter and frontal ventricular enlargement, hippocampal and cingulate gray matter loss.

Symptoms of M.D use that are consistent with psychosis related symptoms which include, visual hallucinations, auditory hallucinations, and persecutory delusions. M.D psychosis recurrence is unique as it recurs without relapse of use.

Chapter 10.

The Detox.

My detox started a few days after getting recalled into a mental health hospital in Stafford, and the withdrawals didn't really start until about 3 days in, I've been here for 17 months now and I'm still feeling the lasting effects now.

For the first 6 months my body was aching I had and still have involuntary movements in my body, my skin was flaky and was rotting away, I was collapsing and passing out due to low blood pressure, my eyelashes and all my hair had fallen out, I was coughing up clots of blood and the pain and discomfort was horrendous the staff here tell me I would lie on a chair made from a leather type material and just shake and move my body out of control to the point where I had worn away the material on the chair. My speech had become fast, and I was getting confused in things I was saying, and I had sores on my legs and feet. I remember I was burning up with a temperature and would sleep on the floor in my room naked by the window splashing myself with water to be able to cool myself down.

As said in previous chapters there was no treatment or replacement the DOCTORS and Nurses could give me all I had was diazepam to try and control the involuntary movements and to relax my muscles that were in a constant aching pain.

To be able to describe the level of discomfort on a rating I couldn't because it would be constantly changing to different parts of my body.

My psyche was also greatly affected I became very paranoid and had aggressive

thoughts and feelings
and had at times
experienced drug
induced "auditory
hallucinations" and
"suicidal thoughts" to
the point where I could
take it any longer and
this along with the
shame of what ide put
my family and loved
ones through I tied a
noose and
contemplated ending
my life before staff
intervened, and self-
harmed by slashing
my torso multiple

time's as a way of distracting myself away from the discomfort I was experiencing, this is something I have never done before and now I'm constantly reminded of the whole thing every time I look at my torso.

Chapter 11.

How I came to be in services.

At 19 I was arrested and convicted for Attempted murder, and kidnap, and was sent to HMYOI Bransford in Wolverhampton. Once arriving at Bransford young offenders from court I immediately was involved in an altercation in the holding room in reception with another inmate and was restrained by prison officers. Once I had been restrained by officers I was taken to ITSU, which the introduction wing, I had previously been in Bransford twice before this so I was already aware of the process and the next day I was moved to E-WING "E 2" and after a hour on the wing I was involved in yet another altercation this time with a prison officer who I had previous running with when I was in Brinsford the last time she was a Scottish lady, if you've been to Bransford around 2006 and earlier you will no doubt know who she is. After this I was moved to "H 1". I had not even had time to clean my pad and go to the toilet before a team of officers escorted me to "H 1".

The first couple of weeks went smooth

on "H 1" and I was trying to keep below the radar as I was aware I was on remand for a serious crime and didn't want to make things worse for myself, and at the time I was already looking at IPP sentence which is a sentence that last's for 99 years and has since been abolished due to the prison system becoming overrun by IPP prisoners. Originally the courts were only meant to hand out 90 IPP sentences to sex offenders of the worst category, but unfortunately people of all offenses were handed an IPP sentence and the system to this day is overcrowded with

IPP'S who are stuck in the system without any hope of getting out.

About a month into my time on "H 1" I took a sex offender hostage in my cell. This didn't last long before officers intervened followed by other incidents of violence on the wing at association times with other prisoners. It got to the point where after setting another prisoner's cell on fire, and trying to set alight to them they sent me down to healthcare for a Mental Health assessment. I didn't realize that this assessment would change the course of my next 16 years. I was subsequently sent to a mental health hospital in Manchester "The Spinney". Once at the spinney I was initially under assessment by both nurses and doctors. Whilst under assessment I noticed my eyesight was deteriorating and I reported this to nurses and doctors at the time but was told I was delusional. After this went on for several weeks and the eyesight deteriorating day by day I started taking sex offenders hostage as a way of protesting to be seen by an optician subsequently leading me to take another 5 hostages over the preceding 6 month period, the final straw was myself and two others taking a member of staff hostage. After this I was referred to "Broadmoor maximum security hospital" who refused me because it was not in my catchment area before finally, I was accepted by "Ashworth high secure" in Liverpool and in 2008 I was transferred there.

June 2008 I arrived at Ashworth, immediately as I arrived, I went through the normal process that I did in prison: a strip search, sitting on the metal detector "boss chair" before having my clothes and belongings taken to be checked and searched. The Ashworth staff tried to make this as invasive as possible. After my initial admission I had a dry come to the ward, I reported my poor eyesight to him and showed him I had red eyes and discharge coming from both eyes, the Dr said this was hay fever and that I was at

the time suffering
from psychosis, and
in fact the eye sight
was a delusion, he
then offered me
antipsychotic
medication which I
refused and threw
the medication on
floor, The staff
came to restrain me
so assaulted the
staff who came and
under restraint they
administered
medication through

a "I.M" injection before locking me in a seclusion room with a toilet and shower and a seclusion bed made out of plastic.
I remained in this room for about a month before slowly being integrated into the ward and every time I complained about my eyes, I was told to take medication

which again led to me assaulting staff and being injected again and taken back to seclusion. Once my mother, and brother Scott were cleared to visit me I was put on closed visits where you see your visitors behind a piece of glass and even with thick glass between us, they had two staff sit in the room writing down everything that was said. The Dr said that this was down to the Hospital protecting my visitors as I was violent and unpredictable because of a delusion I had about becoming blind "laughable really."

Chapter 12.

My quest to plead sanity, and life at Ashworth.

Whilst at Ashworth from the years (2008/2014) I felt as though I was in a constant battle with the system to try and persuade Dr's that even though a person is under section in a mental health facility, that physical health can't be overlooked, and all the emphasis put on mental health. If I was listened to at the time, they would have taken me seriously including my time at the spinney totaling nine years to get an eye test. By that point when I was diagnosed at set Paul's eye hospital in Liverpool the professor seeing me said it was the most advanced case he had seen. After seeing the professor, he informed me that I would need to have a cornea transplant in both eyes, but whilst I waited for a donor, I would have to have intact inserted into

both eyes. Intakes
"are plastic
segments" that look
to bend the cornea
back into its normal
shape, which I
remember being a
very painful recovery
more so than the
graft itself later.

Even after my
diagnosis and first set
of treatments I was
still told my eyesight
problems were in my
head, and I was

delusional. I remember the Dr's at the time at Ashworth speaking to my mother and telling her I was an acute psychotic state and asked her to try and convince me to go onto a antipsychotic call clozapine, which is a powerful anti-psychotic that is used as a last result when a patient is resistant to other medication. Clozapine causes a person's white blood cells to die off and increases risk of infection and heart attack along with excessive weight gain leading to things like diabetes and high blood pressure. I was adamant that this was not a path I wanted to go down and still stayed true to my word, that I was not psychotic.

Eventually I had my first cornea graft, first in my left eye and when I woke up from surgery I was handcuffed to a bed and a member, and 5 other Ashworth staff sat in the room also. I remember saying to the staff do you believe me now to which they replied "no your barking mad lad" I was in a lot of pain and asked for pain relief and the Dr at the eye hospital was going to give it me and administer morphine but the Ashworth staff said no all I could have was paracetamol. I felt sick and I remember thinking "fuck it" lent over and threw up over the staff I was handcuffed to.

After returning back to Ashworth, I met with a Dr I asked him if he believed what I was saying now, the fact I was going blind and this was not make believe in my mind and I was not psychotic to which he replied " you need to keep taking your medication as I believe this is a delusion and at the present time I'm suffering from an acute psychotic illness". I couldn't believe what I was hearing. I didn't believe it after I received a diagnosis and now after my second lot of surgery, they were still telling me it wasn't real, and it was in my mind.

I spent the next 5 years trying to convince a system that knew deep down that there was a miscarriage of justice and in fact I was not psychotic, this was not treatment but rather containment and that H.M.Prison service had enough of me and in fact it was easier to leave me a high security mental health hospital to rot away rather than deal with the issue.

I spent 6 years at Ashworth constantly trying whatever I could to convince the Drs that I was of

compos mentos and
of sound mind.

I spent years
surrounded by some
of the country's most
high-profile offenders
some of whom have
committed horrifying
sexual crimes, and
although I admit I was
in fact incarcerated
for a serious crime
still I was not
suffering from a
mental health
problem or disorder.

It may seem that the ending chapters of this book are in fact going back to the past where I started in the present, but I intend to emphasize to professionals reading this; they can't overlook physical health problems and always put the emphasis on mental health when in fact, some people who say that experience problems that can't be seen with the naked eye much the same way as mental health should be investigated also, not only for the patients care and treatment but also for peace of mind of the person which they are treating.

I appreciate that mental health comes with its complexities

and treatment can be very hit and miss, but a person's journey should always be met with that of emotional caution and in fact by allowing an individual to be led to believe that he/she is suffering from a mental health crises when they are not in itself a very callous way of treating somebody who was more of a management problem in community, and custodial setting, and by putting someone in hospital receiving medication that alters the chemical activity in the brain in fact has a very detrimental impact on an individual's life, both emotionally and biologically.

I didn't get released from hospital altogether from the years of 2006/2022, all the time being led to believe that I was delusional when in fact I was suffering from a physical not mental health problem, has left me deeply traumatized and now unable to cope with life in the community.

Chapter13.

Institutionaliza tion.

After being incarcerated for 16 years I struggled terribly in the community.

I found day to day very difficult things such as walking my dog, going to a restaurant, being out at night which was made worse because of my eye condition as I find it difficult to see in the dark. I had expected to find these things hard but the things I didn't expect to be challenging were sleeping on a bed that was too comfy or getting a bath even when going into my shower taking something with me to protect myself. By biggest savior was my Dog Bella, she helps me have some purpose taking care of her she was and still is my little sidekick.

Feeling this way in the community and always being on edge, and not really feeling as though I fitted in was, I believe the amount of time I had spent locked up, often with long periods of isolation.

Look for things in the community to reinforce thoughts I had in mind that I wasn't good enough for community life. I felt rejected by society so I would reject everything and everyone as a way of compulsively behaving. Friends and family would tell me I had become very impulsive but in fact it was the total opposite I felt I had no control so would act compulsively which was often viewed as impulsive, but these behaviors had that of a safety element to them as at the time I felt out of control experiencing emotional dysregulation, erratic thought patterns, feeling that were intense and out of control, and psychologically, thus behaving in the compulsive ways in which I did gave me a sense of control " reject before being rejected" or "mirror and project negative feelings of self onto someone else to make them feel the same."

These behaviors often led me to live erratically, leading me in dissocial ways of living, for instance

taking drugs,
drinking, fighting etc.

In August 2002 I
accepted Islam I took
my shahada and
became Muslim.

Since becoming
Muslim I found peace
in myself and have
become more
understanding of
other people,
broadening my ability
to think rationally and

be more open to others.

I feel as though I've found a purpose in life now, something to drive me forward, which keeps me on the straight path.

I'm in contact with other Brothers a lot that I already knew from Birmingham who through Islam have changed their lives also. A lot were in

gangs and committing crime but now are working with communities working with youth services, and mental health a H.M. Prisoner service to better educate people on Islam and also supporting the young people to live a better more pro social life.
ALHAMDULILLAH.

A Lot of people when in a dark place will look for some form of peace especially when in hospital or prison. Islam teaches peace and devotion to one God ALLAH. The word Islam itself means peace and devotion, and everyone I know who now accepts Islam have found peace in the darkest of places.

Muslim Brothers/Sister get a lot of bad press and are not really given a chance because of their chosen faith much the same way as I was not given a choice and was branded insane in the system. As I've said in previous chapters about not having a voice and not being accepted left me in a very dark place so by people treating me

with brotherly love
and accepting me for
who I now am as a
Muslim I have found
peace in myself and
turned my life around.

Never let what's
around you determine
how you feel about
yourself, and we all
deserve a chance at
being happy. My
chance was Islam
that's my drive and
purpose, find yours,
love yourself and

naturally others will follow.

ZANE HUNT!!!!!

(09/06/2024)

Printed in Great Britain
by Amazon

43138644R00086